The Gospel According to Les Misérables

30 Devotions to Inspire Faith

Selena Sarns

(with Heather Nordeman)

The Gospel According to Les Misérables: 30 Devotions to Inspire Faith

© 2013 TheBiblePeople.com

Unless marked, Scripture quotations are taken from the King James Version of the Bible.

Cover image of Cosette was drawn by Emile Baynard in 1862 for the first edition of Les Miserables. It is public domain. Source: Commons. Wikimedia

Published by TheBiblePeople.com. Our mission is to encourage people to read, understand, and apply the Bible.

Printed in the United States of America.

Contents

Reading 1
When We Experience Love, it is Easier to Love Another

Jude 22 *"Of some having compassion, making a difference."*

MONSIEUR BIENVENU IS the epitome of graciousness. Known also as Bishop Myriel, this man knows how to exhibit compassion and grace towards others that need it the most. He is a man not soon driven to be impressed by someone's status, as much as he is by their need or condition. This is proven when he opens his home to Jean Valjean, a recently released convict from prison. Valjean has known nothing but misery and hardship, and has the appearance of a rogue. But, true to his nature, Myriel allows Valjean a place to stay and a bed to sleep in. He also spares no expense and makes sure that Valjean is content with food. The Bishop neither asks nor expects anything in return. He simply is showing a loving attitude towards someone that has practically nothing in this world. Compassion towards his fellow man is a hallmark of a true gentleman, and Bishop Myriel is recognized as such.

Have you ever felt that someone was not as loving in their attitude towards you as you had hoped them to be? We all face that at times. However, as Christians, we are to look past the trappings and attitudes of others and simply supply a loving countenance towards them. Whether they treat us with respect or disdain, believers have to exemplify the second of the great commandments, which is to love others as God has loved us. We are not to disconnect from other brethren or the world and pretend that they do not exist. If anything, we should see others the way God sees us and show them an open hand policy of *phileo*, or godly affection.

We should see
others the way god
sees us and show
them an open hand
policy of phileo, or
godly affection.

Reading 2
A Soul is Worth More than Two Candlesticks

Galatians 3:13 *"Christ hath redeemed us from the curse of the law, being made a curse for us..."*

VALJEAN IS REALLY not so different from any of us. We may not be thieves, but we all have sin in our lives that can take the shape of many a transgression against God. Compare our relationship with Christ to how Valjean relates to Bishop Myriel of Digne. Valjean is finally released from incarceration after 19 long years, for having stolen bread and trying to escape. The problem is that Valjean now carries a multitude of character issues from his time in prison. He is discouraged, angry, moody, and full of turmoil. So, his entry back into society is fraught with problems. But, Bishop Myriel (Monsignor Bienvenu, which means to welcome) allows Valjean to stay at his home. He shows Valjean mercy and kindness, without thought of recompense. Valjean shows his "gratitude" by stealing from the benevolent gentleman and running off. When Valjean is apprehended and returned, the Bishop simply tells the authorities that Valjean was given the items and even says that Valjean "forgot the two candlesticks" to take with him. Afterwards, the Bishops says to Valjean, "You no longer belong to evil, but to good. It is your soul I am buying for you. I withdraw it from the dark thoughts and from the spirit of perdition, and I give it to God!" Valjean begins to accept this show of kindness.

Jesus is no different towards us, a humanity that is fallen and carries the curse of Adam. We are sinners, full of discouragement, anger, and turmoil. Our "prison" of sin and regret drives us forward in our lives of despair and disappointment. Yet, the Most High Jesus Christ gives us more than candlesticks; he gives us life eternal by his redemptive work upon Calvary's cross. His blood shed for us tells the Lord that we no longer belong to evil, but to good. It is a personal relationship and we have to accept his gifts of forgiveness and mercy. We can see that Jesus gave His very life for us and gives us the power to overthrow the penalty of sin.

*It is a personal
relationship and we
have to accept his
gifts of forgiveness
and mercy.*

Reading 3
Our Lives are Not Our Own; We Do Affect Others

Matthew 28:19 *"Go ye therefore, and teach all nations, baptizing them in the name of the Father, and of the Son, and of the Holy Ghost:"*

JEAN VALJEAN SPENT over 19 years in prison and when he is released, he finds that no one is willing to let him stay in their homes or give him a job. His time behind bars may have paid his debt, but society is not willing to forgive or trust him. At least, not until a kind man named Bishop Myriel of Digne (or Monsignor Bienvenu) gives the despairing and angry Valjean a place to rest his head and be fed. The Bishop does all of this with no thought of anything in return. He simply lives what he believes, and opens his heart and home towards the wayward man. Even when ValJean attempts to commit thievery from the benefactor, he is shown mercy and forgiveness. Bishop presents an open-hand policy towards Valjean, with no strings attached. The Bishop has this compassion for Valjean because he believes that the ex-convict no longer belongs to evil, but now belongs to good, and that Valjean's soul is being purchased for God. Valjean slowly begins to see a change in his own heart and life once he leaves the home of Monsignor Bienvenu. He begins a journey of passing on that kindness and true compassion to others, in spite of the pitfalls that await him as he moves along.

God comes to us in our lives in much the same way as the Bishop and Valjean. He sees us as worthy of His mercy, and proved it by sending His own beloved Son to take away our sin. As believers, we are to treat others with the same kind of compassion and heart of love. The Bishop taught the hapless Valjean about agape, or unconditional, love, and how to teach it to others in word and deed. We have the same call to teach God's love with word and deed, and see others come to the Savior This is the Great Commission placed upon us as Christians.

God comes to us in
our lives in much
the same way as the
Bishop and Valjean.

Reading 4
Kindness: More from the Heart

Ephesians 4:32 *"Be kind to one another, tenderhearted, forgiving one another, as God in Christ forgave you."*

VALJEAN COMES INTO Bishop Myriel's life as one that has seen hardness and cruelty. He has spent time in prison for simply stealing a loaf of bread (although stealing is still stealing) and his sentence was extended for trying to escape. When he is finally released, Valjean has spent 19 years behind bars, working the harsh chain gangs that are part of the prison culture in France. When he does come into the open invitation of the Bishop, Valjean is full of mistrust after experiencing the closed doors and denial of work by his fellow Frenchmen. However, the Bishop opens his home and heart to grim Valjean, and shows him what kindness can do when given without strings attached. The Bishop expected nothing in return for his benevolent attitude towards Valjean, except a willingness to accept it. Valjean begins a transformation from a hardened character towards that of a kind person who seeks to do right by others. The amazing result is that the transformation does not take long when Valjean realizes he has kept company with a true visage of kindness.

Kindness for the believer is not anything new; however, it can be something that is not shown as often as it should be. Kindness is not a mere action, but a purposed lifestyle. When we show kindness to others that have not seen much of it, we are opening a door to Christian love. Our fellow man is not someone we are to just supposed to give a warm greeting to, although that is a good beginning. He is someone who we are to ensure is being treated with kind words and actions. Sometimes we meet individuals that rub us the wrong way, and our first thought is to leave their presence or lambaste with a harsh word. However, kindness in God dictates that we forgo our own human response and seek to show God's love towards that person. When we show someone kindness, we are demonstrating our Christian charity.

Kindness is not a mere action, but a purposed lifestyle.

Reading 5
Repentance: Having to Say You're Sorry

Luke 5:32 "I came not to call the righteous, but sinners to repentance."

IN LES MISÉRABLES, we see what literature would call a type of protagonist in Jean Valjean. This hapless character has seen the misery of life, thrust at him by circumstances that makes him a bitter and angry individual. He spends time in prison for committing an act of thievery when he steals bread. His time separated from society would have been shorter than the 19 years, if he had not attempted to escape a number of times. Valjean becomes filled with distrust and resentment towards all of society. He has no problem with taking advantage of others, especially after his release, when no seems to be willing to help him. All, that is, except one person. His soon-to-be benefactor, Bishop Myriel of Digne, treats Valjean with respect, compassion, and true care. This man's heart towards Valjean has a surprising effect. It causes Valjean to reflect and consider his ways. Because of the goodness and kindness of one individual,

Jean Valjean slowly goes through a transformation in his life. He begins to develop a conscience about mistreating others; eventually, altering his whole persona by helping his fellow man. A repentant spirit envelops this once hateful and bitter life, and Valjean walks a new course in his life.

When man discovers the kindness and love that Jesus offers, then he, too, sees a change of heart and life. As humans, we are full of bitterness. We rail against society in our daily decisions and thoughts. This is because we each have a sinful heart; a heart that is full of strife, envy, and evil intent. However, one man (just like it took only one person in Valjean's life) exhibited love and compassion when he gave himself on the Cross of Calvary. Jesus, God's own Son, delivered us from the bondage of sin with His shed blood. When we accept the gift of His ultimate price of love, and are truly repentant, we each begin a change in our lives. Redemption by Jesus transforms us into new creatures. Bought with a price, His blood, we come to a newness of life and seek to show that same love to others. We can't help it, as Jesus has completely redeemed us from sin and its ultimate penalty.

Redemption by Jesus transforms us into new creatures.

Reading 6
Misguided Trust can be Life-Changing

Proverbs 21:30 *"There is no wisdom nor understanding nor counsel against the LORD."*

LES MISÉRABLES HAS a sad cast of characters, and one of the most heart-wrenching is young Fantine, This street-living, working-class woman embodies the typical persona of the low income woman of her time. She has left a home life that is arduous and unloving, to live on the streets of Paris. She also is naïve and prone to make bad decisions. Over time, she falls in love with a young man named Félix Tholomyès. She believes him to be someone that will look after her and offer her security. Eventually, she has a child by this soon-to-be-discovered cad of aristocracy. Félix Tholomyès abandons Fantine, and she is left to care for their child alone. Her lack of judgment does not end there. She knows she cannot care for her daughter, so Fantine leaves her with an innkeeper and his wife, whichwill prove to be a wretched situation for her daughter, Cosette. The people Fantine has chosen to trusts and select to be a part of her life prove to be disastrous, to say the least.

We are not much different. The friends we select can, at times, be less than uplifting or edifying. God tells us that we are to be wise in the choices we make, and not to select friends that will affect our testimonies in the wrong way. Yes, we are to be friendly and seek to have a godly effect on the lives of others, but we are not to become like the world. We must use good judgment and godly wisdom when choosing friends that will build us up in our Christian walk. Jesus worked in many people's lives, but he had just a few close friends--we call them his disciples. When we associate with strong believers we are discipling, as well as being taught ourselves. Making the right choices means we surround ourselves with friends that can only make us stronger in our relationship with the Lord.

*Making
the right choices
means we surround
ourselves with friends
that can only make
us stronger in our
relationship with
the Lord.*

Reading 7
Mistakes Are Meant to Make us Better, Not Bitter.

Psalm 31:24 *"Be of good courage, and he shall strengthen your heart, all ye that hope in the Lord."*

FANTINE'S CHARACTER IS born into the poverty of the French Revolution. Napoleon is on the march, and the economy of France is going through great upheavals. Like everyone, Fantine does not choose how she entered the world. But the choices she makes along the way will fashion much of her life in Paris. She makes the mistake of associating with people that will not create a better situation for her. One of her bad choices is getting mixed up with someone she is charmed by, and she ends up living with him. She becomes pregnant and finds herself alone again, but now with a new life soon to come into the world. She continues to make unwise decisions that affect the path of her life. Her daughter, Cosette, is born and she does whatever she has to do to keep them both alive. She makes the mistake of leaving Cosette with people that end up abusing her and keeping her in poverty. Yet, Fantine continues to hope for things to get better for her family. It isn't until the day she is dying, when she asks a friend, Valjean, to take her daughter and raise her, that she knows she has made a good choice.

We all make decisions that seem right at the time, yet later prove to be mistakes. It is a part of the human condition that people will make decisions that turn out to be less than wise. However, it is what we do with the decisions that can either teach us or fester into despair. As Christians, we are shown by God's example how to turn a wrong decision into something positive. The day each of us made the decision to accept the gift of eternal life offered by Jesus was the day we made the all-time best decision. As believers, we are not exempt from making bad decisions. But, we are blessed with a Holy Spirit that enables us to consider our selections. Something may seem logically acceptable, but is it morally right? Through prayer, we can also turn bad decisions into ones that will glorify God and work towards our betterment. With God, mistakes can be corrected and any life, no matter how difficult, can still glorify Him.

With God, mistakes can be corrected and any life, no matter how difficult, can still glorify Him.

Reading 8
Where is Your Comfort Zone?

Proverbs 21:13 *"Whoever shuts their ears to the cry of the poor will also cry out and not be."*

FANTINE IS AN unfortunate woman that never really had a chance to live outside of the bonds of poverty. She was born into the very depth of it in Napoleon's Paris, during a time of economic hardships with war all around. She is forced to live on the streets and find any way possible to make it through the course of the day. She will do anything necessary to stay alive, even if it means surviving by begging or selling her body in prostitution. She sees no hope for her circumstances, and it only gets harder when she bears a child and now has a daughter to raise alone. People look upon Fantine's situation with disdain and ill-will, and never offer to help her. She is taken advantage of with every opportunity that presents itself. Fantine never stops trying to make things better for herself and her little girl, but people around her do not seem to be willing to offer their assistance, especially those with the financial means to do so.

As Christians, we have a responsibility to others that are suffering. The poor and needy have always existed, and the Christian ethic of helping them has always been there as well. If it means stepping out of our comfort zone to provide for someone down on their luck, then we need to be willing to do so. God blesses us, and He can take away those blessings when we fail to show Christian charity to those less fortunate. Christian charity begins within our heart. Be willing to step out of your comfort zone to go where you are most needed.

As Christians, we have a responsibility to others that are suffering.

Reading 9
The Ways of God Win Every Time

Romans 7:22 *"For I delight in the law of God
after the inward man."*

IN HUGO'S LES Misérables, Inspector Javert is a character of strict adherence to the law. His is an existence that transcends any form of humanity and is disciplined to living, breathing, and exhorting strict statutory completeness. One example is shown in his relationship to Jean Valjean. Valjean is a former criminal and convict that has become a changed man, but hides his identity from Javert. Javert knew Valjean in prison when he,

Javert, was a guard assigned in the same location. Javert has since gone on to become a police inspector, and would have no compunction about returning Valjean to prison if he knew that he was a former criminal. Javert holds to each jot and title of the law--man's law. Unlike others in this tale that exhibit mercy and understanding, Javert treats each person that breaks any portion of statute as a threat, and deems punishment to be in order. He knows nothing of understanding or compassion, and makes sure any infraction is meted with "justice".

Mankind is like Javert in many ways. Often, we try to justify that the "eye for an eye" attitude is fair and right. God has established set principles that we are to live by. His ways are righteous and based upon pure love for His creation, which does not always translate to how man feels his life should be lived. When we seek to follow our own order of things, we fail to realize that God has arranged things in a certain way so that our lives can be filled with joy and peace. It is only when people come to realize that God loves them and wants only His best for them that they come to accept His way of thinking. That comes from a trust in His Son as their Savior, and then living lives that follow God's law. Javert knew nothing of a compassionate spirit, and that is where humans find their biggest conflict: they seek to live a life that is based upon their own "law".

*Mankind is
like Javert in many
ways. Often, we
try to justify that
the "eye for an eye"
attitude is fair
and right.*

Reading 10
Man Can Lead, but We Only Bow Down to God.

Leviticus 19:4 *"Turn ye not unto idols, nor make to yourselves molten gods: I am the LORD your God."*

THE FRENCH REVOLUTION marked a period of change in the world, as governments were divided and conquest seemed on the lips of so many military-minded individuals. The grand Emperor Napoleon is one of these that sought to take and conquer for his country.

Napoleon is marked in history as almost godlike. Besides his own self aggrandizement, Napoleon is shaped with supreme qualities. In Hugo's book, Les Misérables, Napoleon's own men hold him in reverential awe. Even in exile, he is seen as some sort of deity by so many of his fellow countrymen. Possibly due to his many campaigns and victorious returns, Napoleon was endowed with certain traits that made him into some form of a giant among giants. Napoleon was merely a man that had the fortune to be successful in many a battle. Emperor Napoleon commanded an almost religious fervor from those that served him.

Placing someone like Napoleon up in the league of deity is not only blasphemous, it is intolerable. Mankind creates idols out of people and things all the time and we tend to falsely worship these things. An idol in any form that takes a Christian's attention off of God is an abomination. He deserves our "Utmost for His Highest" in the way of regard and reverence. If one wants to bow down, he or she should do so before the throne of grace and seek the will of a loving and sovereign Creator. When we give God His rightful worship, we engage in a closer walk with Him.

Mankind creates idols out of people and things all the time and we tend to falsely worship these things

Reading 11
Rescue is On the Way

Daniel 6:27 *"He delivereth and rescueth, and he worketh signs and wonders in heaven and in earth, who hath delivered Daniel from the power of the lions."*

VALJEAN IS IMPLORED by Fantine to save her daughter, Cosette, from the evil clutches of the Thenardiers, the wicked people who own and operate the local inn. Cosette has been in their "care", but suffers great abuse and mistreatment under their hands. Fantine begs Valjean to remove Cosette and get her to a place of safety. Valjean is already living his life under a new identity and on the run from authorities that want to send him back to prison. Still, he takes the urgency of Cosette's rescue seriously, and through various circumstances affects her rescue. Without regard to his own welfare, Valjean does what others will not do and gets her out of the nefarious hands of the wicked innkeepers. He ends up also raising Cosette when Fantine passes away and there is no one else to look after her.

If we see the need to aid another person and to have

an impact upon their life, we should extend Christian charity and bring aid and comfort to the person having problems. It really does not take much out of our day to see to the need of the person. Do we stop when we see someone on the side of the road with a flat tire or steaming car hood? When a person is facing hard financial times, do we offer what we can, or simply move along? When there is a need, Christians need to come to the rescue. As believers, we can also impact someone for Jesus Christ. Everyone has a definitive need to be saved and know that someone is willing to share the good news of Jesus with them. To impact a life is to see the need and supply the answer.

*To impact a life is
to see the need and
supply the answer.*

Reading 12
To Run from God is to Run in Circles

Daniel 9:9 *"To the Lord our God belong mercies and forgiveness, though we have rebelled against him."*

JEAN VALJEAN CREATES a new identity for himself in the French town of Montreuil-sur-Meras the mayor named Madeleine. As a former convict, Valjean finds that no one will give him work because of the stigma he carries. So to get back into society, he creates this new image and begins his new beginning. However, the police inspector Javert suspects that Madeleine is not who he seems to be, and believes Valjean is the same criminal he knew back in prison when he was a guard. One day, Valjean sees a businessman under a collapsed cart, and he lifts the cart to save the man. Javert witnesses this feat and remembers only one person who had that kind of strength...Valjean. Thus begins the investigation by Javert to prove his suspicions; however, it is met with resistance and doubt as Valjean does all he can to hide his past crimes and identity from the inspector. Valjean stays one step ahead of the Inspector, until a day comes when he can no longer hide. When someone is accused of being Valjean and is sent to trial, Valjean finally admits his true identity and faces his consequences.

We do this in our lives. As sinners, we continue to do what we want and behave however we desire. We run from God and his perfect plan for our lives. Unlike Javert, God sees us and knows who we are. But, we still go about our own lives trying to please ourselves and living contrary to God and His will. However, like Valjean, many people find they can only run and hide for so long, living their own way until discontent and sadness begin to creep in. It is not until each person sees their need for forgiveness from a Holy God that we can know that "peace that passes all understanding". God has one intent for our lives, and that is for us to be wholly living according to His will. The truth be told, the Lord already sees us for who we are. When we realize that running from God is futile and empty; we can know that being open before God is true joy.

When we realize that running from God is futile and empty; we can know that being open before God is true joy.

Reading 13
No Good Deed Goes Unnoticed

Ruth 2:12 *"The LORD recompense thy work,
and a full reward be given thee of the LORD
God of Israel, under whose wings thou art
come to trust."*

IN THE STORY Les Misérables, Jean Valjean is on
the run with Cosette, his adopted daughter, from
Inspector Javert. Valjean has hidden his identity
from everyone by becoming the mayor known as
Madeleine. His ruse had gone unnoticed for some
time and he was able to perform his work of good
deeds. However, Javert had his suspicions and finally
was able to unravel the lie that Valjean created. Thus,
Valjean is forced to leave the city and run to stay ahead
of the Inspector. During the course of their escape,
the duo finds themselves in a dark garden. A man
approaches them and Valjean offers the man money
to stay overnight. Unknown to the fake mayor, the
man is Fauchelvant, the same man who Valjean had
rescued earlier from under the fallen cart. He declines
Valjean's money and offers them safekeeping in the

facility, which is a convent. Fauchelvant recognizes his past benefactor and is simply repaying the good deed shown unto him. Valjean and Cosette are offered a warm abode and he leads them into the convent for a night's rest from their travels.

One of the lessons we all learn when growing up is the Golden Rule. This rule states "do unto others as you would have them do unto you". As a philosophy to live a life, this is sound. However, there is more to it than that. Our very lives for God become a testimony of who He is in our hearts. As believers, we are to live in adherence to God's will, which tells us to love others as He loved us. We show our love by doing good to all men. In word and deed, Christians are to give to others less fortunate, to testify about who God is to those that need the Lord, and to help our fellow man in times of crisis and trouble. When we do these things, and more, we store up for ourselves treasures in Heaven. God has declared that various things we do in His name earns us crowns in Glory. The things we do are not to earn us a place in Heaven; but because of who we are in Christ, we choose to do those good deeds.

Christians are to give to others less fortunate, to testify about who God is to those that need the Lord, and to help our fellow man in times of crisis and trouble.

Reading 14
We Are Never Far from Our Heavenly Father

Proverbs 18:24 *"A man that hath friends must shew himself friendly: and there is a friend that sticketh closer than a brother."*

MARIUS, THE COLONEL under Napoleon, never really knew his father. Marius had been raised by a grandfather, and merely heard things here and there about his father. The sad thing is that Marius never knew if his father was even aware of the life Marius was living or if his father even cared for him. Only when an elderly gentleman named Mabeuf shares certain news with Marius does he realize the extent of his father's concern and care for his son. A church warden from Paris, Mabeuf takes Marius aside at the passing of Marius's father and tells him that his father had always been watching the life of young Marius. Mabeuf instructs Marius that his father had loved him as much as any father could have cared for his own son, but he had always done so from a distance. Though he had never been an immiediate part of Marius's life, his father never failed to stay informed about the life of his son.

God is like that. Even though his presence seems distant and uninvolved, God is completely aware of what is happening to his children. In the lives of believers, God has a total awareness of our needs and makes sure we see His hand at work in our lives. God is closest to us at the times we need Him the most. As the Great Comforter, He knows what we seek and where our hearts are. He is not blind to them, nor is He far off. God's very presence comes to us when we come to Him in prayer and seek his loving embrace. It is comforting to know that His presence is immediate and focused.

He is not blind
to them, nor is He
far off. God's very
presence comes to
us when we come
to Him in prayer
and seek his loving
embrace

Reading 15
True Love is Given by God

I Peter 1:22 *"Seeing ye have purified your souls in obeying the truth through the Spirit unto unfeigned love of the brethren, see that ye love one another with a pure heart fervently:"*

Valjean's adopted daughter learns many lessons in her life as she grows within the walls of the convent. Although her life has been surrounded by loss of her mother and the intrigue of her adopted father's world, she also learns about kindness and beauty within the walls of Petit-Picpus. She also learns to know love when she first sets eyes upon young Marius, an officer in Napoleon's army. Marius also is drawn to the young beauty and his heart is forever hers. These two young people never cross the bounds of complete intimacy, and settle for handholding and nearness to each other. Except for a one-time kiss, they never go any further un-wedded. A quote by the author, Hugo, best displays their innocence towards each other: "Marius felt a barrier, Cosette's purity, and Cosette felt a support, Marius' loyalty," Marius does more than respect the young maiden. He is satisfied with their nearness as he values her and remains chaste in his time around Cosette. Marius holds Cosette with adoration that completes him without the need for physical intimacy.

This relationship that Marius has with Cosette has a two-fold lesson for Christians. We know that God has ordained that physical intimacy is to be saved for marriage. As we show our respect and true love for one another, while saving physical intimacy until marriage, we develop a closer bond built upon God working in us. Our love for one another transcends the physical, and is established upon His holiness. There is a deeper meaning that the relationship from Les Misérables provokes us to understand. As Christians, we are called the bride of Christ. When we come to Jesus, we find what it is to have a pure and chaste relationship with the one who redeemed us from our sins. The Lord shows His bride (Christians) a love that is built upon caring for us with purity and true promise of protection. Jesus' very act upon the cross exemplifies that wholesome love he has for His people. We become satisfied with His presence, as He does ours.

This relationship that Marius has with Cosette has a two-fold lesson for Christians.

Reading 16
It is Better to Stand Alone than to Stand for what is Wrong

Joshua 2:24 *"And the people said unto Joshua, The Lord our God will we serve, and his voice will we obey."*

THE YOUNG MARIUS, a Colonel serving with Napoleon, is a neighbor of a gentleman named Jondrette. They live in the same apartment building and soon become involved in each others affairs. Marius finds out, by witnessing the affair through a crack that separates their living quarters, that Jondrette is planning an act of thievery, and possibly murder, upon Valjean and his adopted daughter, Cosette. Jondrette (later discovered to be a man known as Thenardier, a man that once saved Marius's father's life) has his own daughter, Eponine, bring Valjean and Cosette to their home under the guise of seeking work. Valjean and Cosette are disguised as well, as a man called LeBlanc and a woman named Ursula. Marius recognizes his love, Cosette, and fears for her safety, yet he is hampered from interfering directly due to a sense of loyalty towards his father's benefactor, Thenardier. By a certain act, without harming Jondrette or Eponine, on the part of Marius, Valjean is able to escape the clutches of Jondrette and the arresting officers.

Every believer has to make decisions in their lives that test who they are. One such choice is who we choose as friends, and who we align ourselves with when conflict or disagreement arise. We may be forced to choose between loyalties on certain occasions when we have a connection to both sides of an argument. If we find that someone is in fault, it may be that we have to side with those that are seeking what is best for the individual, even when that person is a close friend. Doing what is right for someone has to be more important than our loyalty or fondness for them. Other times, the conflict is such that Christians are not choosing loyalties, but standing on the side of godly folks. Taking a stand means to lay aside your fear and apprehension and simply do what is necessary and right. Believers cannot always be dictated by their conscience, because we still have a sinful nature. The dictation has to come from what is God's will for the situation, and knowing that we are doing the right thing takes godly wisdom.

Believers cannot always be dictated by their conscience, because we still have a sinful nature.

Reading 17
Saying and Being May Not be the Same Thing

I John 2:4 *"He that saith, I know him, and keepeth not his commandments, is a liar, and the truth is not in him."*

THE THENARDIERS, AKA Jondrettes, are perhaps the vilest and most wicked of characters in the story. These innkeepers, tasked with the care of young Cosette, steal the money given to them for her welfare. He is known to commit acts of thievery and deceit to gain personal wealth. His wife is no angel, either, as she subjects Cosette to mistreatment in their home. Yet, this hapless couple tries to present themselves as God-fearing people that commit charitable acts. Their façade does not fool too many people, but they still try to give an air of piety to their everyday lives when out in public. They are even given to murderous intent, such as when they tried to hold and possibly murder Monsieur LeBlanc and his young charge (who in reality was Valjean and Cosette). They will stoop to any level to commit a crime for their own greed.

To be a Christian is more than simply saying you are so. The fruits of the Spirit need to be present in the life of someone that has accepted the gift of Salvation through Jesus Christ. It is not to say that a person that claims to be saved is not a child of God, but even scripture tells us that deeds follows the profession. That is like someone saying they are a policeman or a doctor; if they do not perform the actions daily of their vocation, it is highly suspect that the individual is not what they claim to be. Salvation through Jesus also creates a new life in a Christian's heart. They want to please God and do His will. The things of the flesh need to be put away. Does it mean that a believer will not commit a sin? No,but it means that through repentance and seeking forgiveness for that thought or action, the Christian seeks to follow what is important in God's heart. Words are all well and good, but if there is no willingness to do good works, the words can fall on empty ears and cause disbelief.

Words are all well and good, but if there is no willingness to do good works, the words can fall on empty ears and cause disbelief.

Reading 18
Sin Can Steal Joy and Blessing

Titus 2:12 *"Teaching us that, denying ungodliness and worldly lusts, we should live soberly, righteously, and godly, in this present world;"*

THE MOST VILE of characters in the book Les Misérables are the Thenardiers. This couple, once innkeepers turned into beggars and thieves, are an example of lives following every sinful practice possible. If they could steal, rob, murder, or devise any nefarious idea to make a quick dollar, then they did it. They were abusive towards a young girl placed in their care, Cosette. They used the money intended for her care for themselves, and created a life of hardship and filth for the young Cosette. Later, the Thenardiers devise a plan to murder Valjean and his young charge, Cosette, but their plans are thwarted and Valjean is able to make his escape. These are the type of people the Thenardiers are. They lack any form of redemptive behavior and are simply out to meet their own personal lusts and greed. The basic fact is they were as sinful a couple as could be found.

Christians are not exempt from sinful thoughts. We still deal with the flesh, but we also have the Holy Spirit to aid us in living lives that seek to flee from sinful lusts. It is one thing as a non-believer to fall prey to the wiles of the evil one that tries to bind hearts to his ways. The ease of making a fast buck, and the desire to own possessions (which in itself is not a bad thing), these all can take our focus off of how we are to live. As Christians, we have a spiritual armor to fight the attacks of Satan and not fall into sin. Other fruits of the flesh can show their ugly heads as well. Covetousness, greed, and hostility are examples of things we are to guard against as Christians. The battle is daily, but through Him we have the means to have daily victory.

Christians are not exempt from sinful thoughts. We still deal with the flesh, but we also have the Holy Spirit to aid us in living lives that seek to flee from sinful lusts.

Reading 19
A Father's Love

John 3:16 *"For God so loved the world, that he gave his only begotten Son, that whoever believes in Him should not perish, but have eternal life."*

JEAN VALJEAN TAKES on a new responsibility in his already harrowed life. In his promise to the dying Fantine, Valjean takes on the responsibility of taking care of her daughter, Cosette. Fantine herself has hardly ever known kindness or mercy. Living on the streets during a majority of her life and plying the trade of a prostitute, hers has been a life of despair and misery. Valjean shows empathy towards the now-dying Fantine and finds himself with Cosette to raise and develop into a good person. She had spent time being "taken care of" by an evil innkeeper and his equally vile wife. She was mistreated and relegated to the role of scullery maid, while the money sent for her care was used by the innkeepers for personal gain. However, under the parenting of her new step-father, Valjean, Cosette finds what it means to know true love by someone and to be well looked after. Her new life is not without trials and pitfalls, because of the situation Valjean is in with keeping his identity secret and being on the run. But, that never keeps him from truly loving his young ward and making sure she is safe.

For the Christian, this same type of love is shown by our heavenly Father. God looks after his children, daily providing for their needs and being available when they need to pray. God's love is unconditional, similar to that of Valjean for his stepdaughter. His love is never ending, just because we might go astray or make stupid decisions. God's ultimate show of love was in sending his Son to shed his blood for the sins of all mankind. He provides a way through Jesus for all to come to Him. That was sacrifice to the highest end; His Son giving His own life so that mankind could trust in Him and spend eternity with Him. Just like fathers make decisions that hurt them personally, they will give their all to make sure their children are loved and cared for. God is no different; in fact, his love is the ultimate show of devotion.

God is no different;
in fact, his love is
the ultimate show of
devotion.

Reading 20
Letting Go is Godly Care

Proverbs 3:5-6 *"Trust in the Lord with all your heart; and lean not upon your own understanding. In all your ways, acknowledge Him, and He shall direct your path."*

EPONINE, THE DAUGHTER of the evil Thenardier, is hopelessly and irrevocably in love with Marius. Marius, a colonel in Napoleon's army, does not share the same sentiment. His heart belongs to the young Cosette. The irony in this saga from Les Misérables is that Eponine and Cosette spent some time together when Cosette was being looked after by her father back at the inn. It is also irony, or fate, that Cosette meets Marius through Eponine.

At first sight, Marius and Cosette are drawn together and fall hopelessly in love. Eponine sees that her affection for the young soldier will not be returned to her, yet she is determined to aid Marius in being reunited with his Cosette.

She is willing to let Marius go, and instead seeks to

help him in his quest for Cosette. Even though it brings her great personal anguish, Eponine does not tell Marius of her love towards him, and puts aside her own wants for his happiness.

We as believers should hold that same value in our lives. God tells each of us, His children, that He is willing to take our yoke upon Himself to make our walk with Him easier. So it should be that, as Christians, we would seek to rid ourselves of our own needs and wants if it means bringing joy or a better situation into the life of another.

Part of the life of a believer is to see others come to Jesus. If we are not willing to let go and give to others, why would someone who is lost want to have what we claim to have through Christ? Putting ourselves aside is more than just a single action or giving up one thing; it is a mindset, a devotion to the One that sacrificed everything for us. Giving up for the best for others is one way believers show the love of an all-giving God.

*If we are not
willing to let go and
give to others, why
would someone
who is lost want to
have what we claim
to have through
Christ?*

Reading 21
The Greatest Sacrifice

John 15:13 *"Greater love hath no man than this, that a man lay down his life for his friends."*

In Les Misérables, many character traits are exemplified through the lives of the individual lives being cast. However, the one trait that is a show of true devotion and love is that of one giving their own life for another. The young Eponine, a waif of a girl and daughter to the evil Thenardiers, is hopelessly in love with someone she can never be with. Marius, the dashing officer under Napoleon's command, has his heart set on another. His is a heart of goodness and compassion towards the girl who was part of a plot to entrap him by her wicked father, but he has no romantic intents towards the young girl. Eponine realizes that she is in love with someone who will never reciprocate the same feelings, yet she does something that fully demonstrates her devotion to Marius. When an opportunity arises for someone to cause harm to the young colonel, she places herself in harm's way for him. She takes a bullet that is meant for Marius, and gives up her own life so that he might live. It is not until her dying breath that Marius fully realizes Eponine's feelings for him and what she has given for his life.

Jesus did that same thing for the world. He left the glory of Heaven to come to earth and shed his blood on the Cross of Calvary for each one of us. Jesus was willing to die, so that mankind had the opportunity to escape the final end for their sin. When each person accepts His ultimate show of love, they gain a gift-- eternal life. That same show of love is a demonstration towards Christians for how they should be willing to sacrifice for others. Most of the time, the thing asked to be sacrificed is not as intense as sacrificing one's life. It may be small things of time and money; however, it may be larger ways of showing love towards another.

She takes a
bullet that is meant
for Marius, and
gives up her own
life so that he
might live.

Reading 22
Doing the Right Thing is Not
Always the Easiest

II Chronicles 20:32 *"And he walked in the way of Asa his father, and departed not from it, doing that which was right in the sight of the LORD."*

JEAN VALJEAN HAS already been living a life marked with tragedy, poor choices, and a social stigma. He has spent time in prison and ends up changing his identity when he is free, so that others will not capture him and return him to a life of confinement. Yet he has faced redemption, when someone took an interest in him as a person and not as a former convict. Valjean learns the value of kindness and compassion when it was displayed towards him by Bishop Myriel of Digne. The prayers and actions of the Bishop begin to have an effect upon Valjean, and he soon learns what it means to live a clean life, even when the circumstances may not be in your favor. When he reaches out to the dying prostitute, Fantine, and promises to raise Fantine's daughter, Cosette, Valjean makes a decision that will affect the rest of his life. The added responsibility undoubtedly will slow down Valjean's escape from those that want to see him back in prison. Yet, he makes the choice to do the right thing in the face of assured hardship, all for the responsibility and blessing of seeing Cosette raised properly and safely.

Doing the right thing sometimes means making decisions that may seem unpopular to others. We may face ridicule and even efforts by others to thwart our purposes. But it is important to continue to move on and do what is right. We may face temptations that seek to move us off of the path of doing right, and these temptations can feel good. But, it is never right to do what is against God's will The most important thing the Christian has is his or her testimony. If you ruin that, you ruin your effectiveness for bringing others to Christ.

Valjean learns the
value of kindness and
compassion when
it was displayed
towards him by
Bishop Myriel of
Digne.

Reading 23
Let God Be the Judge of That

Luke 6:37 *"Judge not, and ye shall not be judged: condemn not, and ye shall not be condemned: forgive, and ye shall be forgiven."*

JEAN VALJEAN SPENT 19 years in prison for stealing bread and attempting to escape a number of times. Those years spent in hard chain gang conditions created a man that was bitter and distrusting of anyone. Upon his release, he found that people were judging him everywhere he went, because of who he was and because he had been in prison. Valjean learns a lesson about human goodness through the efforts of one man named Bishop Myrial of Digne or Monsieur Bienvenu. The Bishop shows kindness towards the hapless ex-convict, who in turn learns what it is to be forgiven, and seeks to make a better way of life for himself. However, police Inspector Javert is not so soon to forgive, and when he realizes that Valjean is out of prison, he seeks to capture him. Javert determines that Valjean needs incarceration and does whatever he can to find him. It does not matter that Valjean has paid his debt to society; Javert sees him as someone that does not deserve freedom, and he seeks to capture him.

Sometimes believers are the first to look at the letter of the law and condemn someone for something, without checking the facts or asking the accused if they are actually guilty of the omission, incident, or crime. God has already established the rules for how we are to relate to others. The old saying, "the pot calling the kettle black" has considerable merit when it comes to how Christians deal with other people. We see someone in a sin, or appearance of such sin, and automatically judge them as guilty for the crime. If we cannot claim the truth of God's Word when he says He executes justice on the evildoers, where do we think we can do better? The answer is simple. We cannot. We are to work with our brethren when they are in fault, but we are not to be judge and jury. If they continue to resist our help, God will declare the final answer.

Sometimes believers are the first to look at the letter of the law and condemn someone for something, without checking the facts or asking the accused if they are actually guilty

Reading 24
So Many Around Us
Have Needs, Too

Philippians 2:4 *"Let each of you look not only to his own interests, but also to the interests of others."*

FANTINE WAS DYING and needed someone to come to her help. She had major concern for the ultimate welfare of her only child, Cosette. Life had not been good to Fantine, and she had lived more days in anguish than she could ever remember. However, her one joy was in her daughter, and she did not want to pass away knowing her daughter had no one to look after her. Valjean came to the rescue of the ailing street dweller. Having lived a life imprisoned and on the run from those that would destroy his freedom, Valjean could have thought of his own needs and moved on. But Fantine was his friend and he felt the need to help her and to allow her peace in her passing. His demeanor becomes embroiled with a new way of thinking, and he soon becomes involved in other people's lives. Even though he has taken on a new identity to keep his pursuers at bay, his countenance has not gone awry. Valjean becomes guardian to the young Cosette and lives his life to ensure her safety and that she would grow up in a loving environment; something her own mother had never known. Valjean places his own needs second to those of another.

Believers are much the same way. When they come to know Jesus as their personal Savior, they find new joy and see change in their hearts. What once would have been a life lived to gain all they can get is now one that seeks to help others. Being a Christian is not just saying, "be filled and be warmed". It is a life devoted to meeting the needs of others, even when personal space or comfort is being imposed upon. Doing things for others is dedication to show the love of someone that gave up His own well-being for our salvation. In other words, living for others is living as an imprint of Christ.

*Believers are much
the same way.*

Reading 25
Do unto Others
Is Not Simply Something We
Merely Say…We Do It

Colossians 3:14 *"And above all these
things put on charity, which is the bond of
perfectness."*

IN LES MISÉRABLES, Jean Valjean has spent much
of the story escaping the persistent Inspector Javert.
Javert knew of Valjean back in prison, and when he
sees Valjean free he is determined to apprehend him.
Javert is a man of the law, to the strictest letter, and
does not believe Valjean can be allowed to be left
free in society. He is convinced that Valjean must
pay for his crimes (even though he has already done
so). So to escape, Valjean has changed his identity a
few times to try and throw the inspector off of his
trail. This treatment would have made the old Valjean
bitter, and he would have wanted to seek to become
the hunter and destroy his nemesis. But much has
changed in Valjean through redemption and love
for a young charge, Cosette. Thus, when opportunity

presents itself to kill Javert, he does the only good thing--he allows him to go free. He shows mercy towards someone that has not given Valjean the same courtesy. The heart of Valjean has been softened and changed to kindness.

God showed mercy upon us when He gave His only begotten Son, Jesus, to hang on a cross on Calvary for all of mankind. He spared us from eternal separation from Himself by keeping us from the eternal damnation that we deserve. His mercy extends to all that simply trust in the redemptive work of His Son, Jesus. So how, as believers, do we perform any less of an act of kindness when opportunity presents itself? If we see a need, we are to be there to fill it. When someone is taken with a hurt or personal problem, our first thought should be to pray for them and to do what we can to ease their pain. Carnal man calls it passing it forward; God calls it Christian love or charity. If someone slights us, we need to be forgiving of the trespass. There is righteous anger over sin, but not anger towards someone we feel did us wrong. We have to rise above our human pride and remember what Jesus did for us.

If someone slights us, we need to be forgiving of the trespass

Reading 26
Giving To Others From What God Has Given Us

II Corinthians 8:5 *"And this they did, not as we hoped, but first gave their own selves to the Lord, and unto us by the will of God."*

V ALJEAN HAS A responsibility in raising Cosette. At one time, he had the impressive opportunity of being the mayor, until his identity was breached by a local police inspector.

But as he has been on the run, he finds he must keep his identity low-key. It becomes apparent to him that he must be of the lowly side of society or risk closer scrutiny by those that would see him apprehended. He becomes a beggar and seeks to gain financial help through this means. However, Valjean is not remiss in giving of what he has towards others in need as well. Often times he would go out, sometimes with Cosette at his side, and drop money into the hands of another street person for their own benefit. He soon is known as the "beggar who gives alms". Valjean does not forget where he came from, and has the philanthropic heart to try and ease the misery of others by giving them money.

"To give is better than to receive" is the way most of us have been taught. That godly principle is even truer with Christians. God did not withhold from us by providing us with salvation; so we should not be slothful to help others as we have supply to do so. We see the homeless around us or the local shelters can use volunteer help, and so we can give to those less fortunate. Charity is not something we only believe, but it is something we take steps to perform. Not only are we showing the light of Christ when we give of ourselves, we are making someone else's life a bit easier. It isn't even that we are thinking we are changing the world, but that we are having an effect in the life of that one person. Too often, people will see those in need and simply walk on by, but as believers we see with new eyes filled with compassion. Truly, to give is better than to receive.

Too often, people will see those in need and simply walk on by, but as believers we see with new eyes filled with compassion. Truly, to give is better than to receive.

Reading 27
It Is Never Too Late

II Peter 3:9 *"The Lord is not slack concerning his promise, as some men count slackness; but is longsuffering to us-ward, not willing that any should perish, but that all should come to repentance."*

A LIFE SPENT IN prison for stealing bread. Then extra years added to his hardship for the attempted escapes and beating of another person. Such was the life of Valjean in Les Misérables. This man is now an adult, and has spent a major portion of his life in degradation and misery, surrounded by every vile and wicked segment of society. He has not known much in the way of happiness and beauty. However, that begins to change after he meets the Bishop Myriel who takes Valjean in and shows him godly charity. After this meeting and subsequent lessons in compassion, Valjean begins to go through a transformation in his own life. New trials present themselves when he changes his identity and begins a fugitive life running from those that would seek his apprehension or death. He makes friends along the way, and is responsible for another life, the young Cosette. Her mother has passed away and he takes Cosette under his wing to raise her and keep her safe. Other events take place that would harden others, but Valjean sees things anew and as the years roll along, his heart is changed towards goodness and love. Redemption fully comes to the character of Valjean as he nears the end of his life.

Sometimes people that come to the Lord Jesus do so in later years in their lives. They may have been raised in a Christian home, but never opened their heart toward Him until they were adults. Some of us may be in our 40s or even 70s before we trust in Jesus and what he did for us on the Cross. Young people that accept Christ as their Savior early on have an amazing opportunity as they grow and become discipled. However, that does not mean that salvation is for just those that come to Jesus by a certain age. There have been times when Christ became someone's salvation at the point just before their passing.

The amazing thing about Jesus' blood and the Cross is that it knows no age limit.

The amazing thing about Jesus' blood and the Cross is that it knows no age limit.

Reading 28
Confession is Good for More Than the Soul

I John 1:9 *"If we confess our sins, he is faithful and just to forgive us our sins, and to cleanse us from all unrighteousness."*

VALJEAN HAS A lived a full life and is now near death. Years ago, he gained redemption and shared with Bishop Myriel of Digne that he would live his life according to the lessons the Bishop has taught him. Although assuaged by guilt along the way and various trials that plagued him, Valjean has lived according to that promise he made so long ago. Upon his deathbed, his face is lit only by the same candlesticks that Myriel gave him at the story's beginning. Valjean's young stepdaughter, Cosette, and Marius come to see him upon his deathbed. It is in this setting that Valjean finally reveals everything about himself, his past, and who Cosette's mother was, to the young couple. He confesses to Marius of his past crimes and asks both of the young people for forgiveness towards him and his deception. Although he had kept the truth from Cosette for good reason, he still feels he needs to be open and ask for forgiveness. Valjean realizes that more is at stake here, and he uses the time as a lesson for the couple about forgiveness.

It can not be said enough that forgiveness is one of the most important intangibles in the life of a Christian. First off, it is the fruit of the Spirit that was shown towards us at the Cross. God forgives us our sins when we accept Jesus as our savior. Then he continues to forgive as we seek His forgiveness when we fall short and sin as believers. So, if someone commits a transgression towards us, we are to be forgiving as well. Jesus forgave many during His earthly life. His life is an example towards Christians and non-believers alike. Sometimes we see people that we know are not Christians show forgiveness, so how much more should a believer show the same? "To err is human, to forgive is divine".

*It can not be
said enough that
forgiveness is one of
the most important
intangibles in the life
of a Christian.*

Reading 29
You Can Change Your Name, Not Who You Are

I Corinthians 8:6 *"But to us there is but one God, the Father, of whom are all things, and we in him; and one Lord Jesus Christ, by whom are all things, and we by him."*

VALJEAN, IN HIS staying ahead of Inspector Javert, knew he needed to change his identity. By doing so, people would forget who Valjean was, and think of him as someone new. He took on the name Madeleine when he became the mayor of the small village. Javert still thought that this man was the infamous Valjean, but it still placed a cloud of doubt in his thinking and made him wonder if that was true. But the need arose for Valjean to change his name again, so he took on the moniker Monsieur LeBlanc. By having this new name with Cosette in his life, Valjean sought to create more distance between him and the authorities. Other characters in Les Misérables alter their identity to obscure the facts. For example, the wicked couple, the Thenardiers, became the Jondrettes. They have handled the inn for so long that, now that they are on the move, they create a facade for themselves. However, the name change does not change their wicked hearts.

Sometimes Christians are that way in their own identities. It isn't that they change their names, but they alter how they appear to different people in their lives. It may be they do not want to offend those they work with, so they act like the rest of the office--by laughing at the dirty jokes or associating with situations that would affect their testimony. Yet, come Sunday, they fill the pews and lead the music at church with no one the wiser. Or so they think; but God sees their heart. Young believers can be that way as well. They are the epitome of Christian action at home, but with their friends, peer pressure wins. We just have to realize that God changed our lives for a reason when we became His through Jesus' blood. Jesus already felt the shame having His Father turn His back on Him when Christ was upon the cross. Believers do not have to lack boldness to be who they are--the Spirit can help with that.

Believers do not
have to lack boldness
to be who they are-
-the Spirit can help
with that.

Reading 30
The Fight is Led and
Conquered by God

Ephesians 6:12 *"For we wrestle not against flesh and blood, but against principalities, against powers, against the rulers of the darkness of this world, against spiritual wickedness in high places."*

LES MISÉRABLES IS an intricate story full of individual stories. The book by Victor Hugo is set in a time when France is in great turmoil as a nation, as it is in the midst of warfare, with Napoleon leading the military, and with poor economic conditions. Times are hard and people are feeling forced to do things they might not do if times were better. The squalor and poverty of France is shown in the lives of many individuals. Jean Valjean does time in prison for theft and attempted escape, and upon his release finds he cannot find a place to stay or work. When kindness is shown to him he responds by stealing again, until the goodness of another begins to work in his own heart. Others, such as a young woman Fantine, live on the streets, begging and falling prey to every lie and deceit present. Her choices cause her to fall further into gloom and sorrow. Thieves are everywhere, as in the characterization of Jondrette and his daughter Eponine, who once ran a successful inn and now languish in poverty. They resort to all types of evil and deceit, driven by their greed. Jondrette is also willing to commit murder to gain what he wants. He has no compunction about taking a life, if it makes his own life more palatable. Les Misérables contains a myriad of characters with their own issues and fallibilities. Each individual intertwines with the others, and conflict ensues.

The story of Les Misérables is not so far removed from a Christian's life. Each one of us faces similar temptations and conflicts that impact who we are in Christ. The spiritual realm is in attack mode all the time. Each fruit of the Spirit becomes a necessary defense against the lust of the flesh. Through suffering we can battle anger, and greed can be fended off by being satisfied with what God gives us. Ephesians 6 describes how believers have a suit of armor that is a defense against the attacks of the evil one. The only offensive piece of the armor is the Sword of the Spirit, and that works best when we are girded with the rest of God's spiritual armor. Interestingly, the only part of the body not protected is our backs, based upon the description of each armor piece. That means we have the means to face the enemy and never have to be on the retreat. As Valjean grew in his knowledge of goodness and redemption due to the kindness shown him, believers grow in their walk by the Grace of Christ shown unto them.

The story of Les Misérables is not so far removed from a Christian's life. Each one of us faces similar temptations and conflicts that impact who we are in Christ.

ABOUT THE PUBLISHER

TheBiblePeople.com exists to help people read, understand, and apply the Bible.

Facebook.com/TheBiblePeople